THE ECSTASY
OF THE
FIRST KISS

Abby Nouri

VANTAGE PRESS
New York

FIRST EDITION

Copyright © 1992 by Abby Nouri

Published by Vantage Press, Inc.
516 West 34th Street, New York, New York 10001

Manufactured in the United States of America
ISBN: 0-533-09580-8

Library of Congress Catalog Card No.: 91-90890

0 9 8 7 6 5 4 3 2 1

WITH LOVE . . .

To my wise and beautiful wife, Ada,
for the fifty years of strength, courage, support,
and happiness she has shared with me
and for being the inspiration for much of my creative work

Contents

Introduction

It is my father, who shared with me his own love of literature and all the creative arts, to whom I owe the greatest thanks. Because of him I have spent a lifetime enjoying literature, philosophy, and art, and recording my thoughts and images on paper. As years passed, I have written literally hundreds of poems and stories until now, in my seventy-fifth year, I have decided to share my work with the public. So it is, I give you this collection of poems, chosen from among many. Hopefully, you will enjoy reading them as I have enjoyed writing them.

Abby Nouri
March 1, 1991

Acknowledgments

Preparation and publication of this book would not have been possible without the commitment and assistance of my son, Shawn, and my daughter-in-law, Donna. I am greatly indebted to them for the invaluable help they gave at every stage.

Sphere of Life

At dawn in a trance-like state, I saw myself enter the
     sphere of life.
It was a huge scalene crystal ball with many sides and
     angles.
There were two, three, four, five magi or more in dazzling
     colors,
All meditating, sitting or standing in each angle.

There could be heard a cacophony of incantations from
     each angle.

One magus was reciting to his beads, "Life is circular,
     repetition upon repetition."
Another was telling his beads, "Life is the unending
     rippling of time, a chain of fractions of moments that
     continues to infinity."
And another, "With every glimpse and movement there is
     a new view, a new sun and light, each complete unto
     itself."

There were an infinite number of these incantations . . .

I learned that to be eternal is to listen and learn, to tell and
     teach,
And to allow absorption so to be able to offer reflection.

Hope

Hope,
Oh, you, the comfort of hearts and the promise of triumph.

Hope,
Oh, you, the word that means living, health, survival, and
   longevity.
How is it that the hopeful person is ever prosperous and
   content, even though faced with difficulties?

Hope,
It is a fact that contemporary man lives for his hopes, and
   his hopes make him live.
Just as breathing and the orderly circulation of blood
   guarantee life, so do hope and optimism.
Therefore, Heaven! Would that to the last moment of life
   we don't forget this sacred name, and the nightmare
   of hopelessness and despair never comes to us.
And, Heaven! Would that the happy and sweet face of life
   and living manifest itself always.
And may the hopefulness of a deep faith in one's own
   endeavors and lofty purpose, in the support and
   friendship of others, in the assistance of fortune,
And in any other agreeable element always surround the
   hopeful man, making a halo of light.

Passage of Time

Although every day is the turning of time
With all manner of change in life,
Still, time is the spreader of thoughts,
And divulger of secrets,
The creator of many impressions.

Although every part of the seasons brings
Change and new conditions,
As time goes by it is also
The maker of new things,
Mixer of elements and recycler of all waste.

Although this passage of years,
Months, days, hours, and seconds, of time itself,
Is as if on the road to banishment,
Always burning at its own existence,
It still has plentiful effects on the universe
And all living things,
Even though it may create complicated
And long-lasting problems.

Alas! That influential scholars and powerful leaders,
     learned people, and pretending religious preachers
Have kept the seal of silence.

Alas! What if this passage of time was really
A path to serendipity and growth
Along the line for each person?
Even a very tiny stone thrown into the water
Will create a circle of waves for a long time.

Then how can we believe our individual efforts
Will not have any effects on change
In the course of time and in its passage?

Chain

Farewell, as you disappear from the face of the earth, You,
    O Chain.
A thousand million groans and curses echo after You,
    O Chain.
Enraged faces and hearts and minds filled with bitterness
    and hatred
Block your rocky and uneven route to disappearance, You,
    O Chain.

There exists for you no single supporter or friend.
None have seen but force, constraint or anger from
    You, O Chain.

From the moment your raw metallic ore was brought from
    the mine,
How many times have you changed your color or adapted
    your form?
From the time you first became a collar, how many animals
Have you tormented, cruelly tortured, and moved around,
    You, O Chain?

You are the powerful means that brought the fearless
    lion
From the thicket, as though a tongue-tied sheep, You,
    O Chain.

Some in history have put you to work in the name of
    Justice,
But those very few, so-called just, moments can be likened
    to the
Instances when a few of the trees and plants send forth
    early buds,
Premature signs of Life, here and gone before the true
    advent of Spring.

    With your coarse, awkward rings; your rude, ugly
        character,
    How can any person rely on or trust You, O Chain?

You have bound so tightly the hands and feet of the weak
    and powerless.
At times you lashed out at them, flogging and whipping
    them, You, O Chain.
In the hands of wicked men you have been used as an
    instrument
Of torture, defiling the value of their women, You, O Chain.

    In farms and factories, schools and homes, you have
        been a source
    Of tears for the innocent, delicate child, You, O Chain.

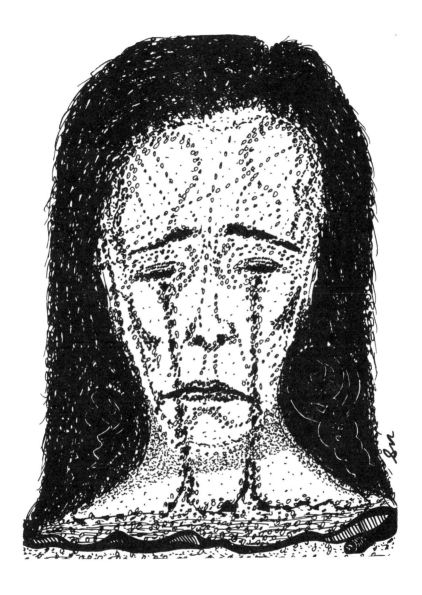

You have been a heavy exploiter on the backs of the
     virtuous,
By your weight bringing them to subjugation, You,
     O Chain.
In the hands of the more powerful, you have been used to
     capture
Defeated armies, and to hold their soldiers helpless, You,
     O Chain.

     Row upon row of innocent men, women and children
     Have been held as slaves in your shackles, You,
          O Chain.

Even when made of gold, shaped into an enviable
     necklace, and
Worn by a sweetheart as an ornament of love, You,
     O Chain,
You are the same. How do they differ—feet from head, hat
     from kerchief?
It matters not gold or iron; both prove ownership with
     You, O Chain.

Since both restrain rather than free, then oppression of
The soul, the mind, or the body is the same, O Chain.

The wise have said a world based on cruelty cannot
    endure, O Chain.
Neither will a world of slavery, injustice and inequality.
Preparations have begun. Help is coming from all
    directions
To rescue the world from the bonds of your oppression,
    You, O Chain.

The end to slavery has come. The hands of humanity
Stretch forth to receive kindness and service, O Chain.

Since movement has been given to machinery, the beasts
    have been
Freed of their burdens and captivity under You, O Chain.
Since women now adorn themselves with knowledge and
    expertise in
The sciences, we can look at you as something inferior,
    You, O Chain.

Everywhere the people are bravely rejecting you.
The reign of power is out of your hands, You,
    O Chain.

For these many reasons I can see you becoming
    fragmented.
The resentment toward you is universal, You, O Chain.
Still, there are those who would make you a tool of
    peaceful purposes,
But to me this a very unlikely role for You, O Chain.

    Yes, the age for evil and exploitation has ended.
    There will remain no sign except You, yourself,
        O Chain.

My Sweetheart's Beauty

The other night during a deep sleep, I dreamed of my
sweetheart's beauty.

I knelt before her with mixed feelings of rapture, ecstasy,
humility, and condescension.

As soon as my tongue wanted to speak of the pain of
separation,

I silenced it, and spoke instead of the sweet, beautiful
feeling she brings.

Suddenly, I was transformed into dust covering a large
area on and away from which she began to walk.

Then I was alone, questioning whether the lonely heart
was so worthy of acclaim.

In all the universe there is no image such as hers, or even
one with the slightest similarity.

Her very likeness will create a new religion in the most
devout person.

It is pure and celestial so as to be inconceivable to the
minds and the understanding of the wise.

With any training and profession, and any investigation or
verification,

These are testimony for describing the power and truth of
knowledge.

It was in her character, such a sense of creation,

And in her existence, as a reason or means for honesty and
purity of action and thought.

There is no way any impostor sowing discord could reach
her.

I thought to myself, even though I might perish in her way,

I was hearing this, permanence and eternity, felicity and
grace, and I was picking the flower of true love.

The Wonders of Her Stature

O God, why have you created in my sweetheart's eyes
    such a sensuousness?

Her glance, so penetrating and attractive; her mouth, a
    gem that speaks without talking;

Her lips, so harmonious and moist.

Why have you made her face so beautiful, with skin like a
    petal from the most delicate flower?

Her stature compares to that of an erect cypress tree. Why
    have you created such grace?

You taught her hundreds of ways to be coquettish,
    amorous, and playful,

And you created me for supplication.

Why have you created a cruciform of her hair that is so
penetrating it is killing to me?

As a result, you have mired and kneaded me into relish,
gusto, and sentiment,

And you created her jovial, charming, and fascinating.

O God, don't take these doubts and questions as impiety.

It's just that you have created both the cup bearer and the
wine.

It was also you who created both Joseph and Mary,

And hundreds and thousands of lovers, like Romeo and
Juliet.

Clear Sky

Oh, mountains and valleys cave in; Oh, hills roll into the
    ditches.
Oh, trees. Oh, elevations. Oh, roughnesses.

All will be overturned into the depressions,
Until there are no obstacles left in the way of the sky.

Nothing or nobody can cover the azure blue of the
    heavenly sphere;
And the world with all its brightness and glory can be seen
    everywhere by everybody.

Isn't it true that broad spacious thinking requires
    far-reaching vision?
Or maybe expanded vision needs unlimited space?

When the signs of hatred, spite, revenge, or any of life's
    foulness have all disappeared,
What else can remain but the star-filled open sky
That to infinity carries purity, clarity, and Peace.

Law

Law,
You, who to everyone seem to be so obvious and so clear.
Order is the result of law.

Question,
Some consider you a necessity for every walk of life.
Some consider you an obstacle to all their intentions and
　　life.

Law,
You, who messengers to politicians alike lay claim to your
　　order in their books and in their manifestos.
Who by great thinkers, in giving guidance for harmony
　　and better living, are seen as vital to humanity for
　　orderly and just living.

But,
What a pity that all people in all times consider you eternal
　　in each case, some see you as myth to be followed
　　blindly, regardless of religious order, political system,
　　or philosophy.

Also,
For their own reasons some even see you as a
　　contradiction to science and progress, knowledge,
　　change, and human needs;
Even a contradiction to evolution.

Law,
Even in the natural world and universe with its purity and
naturalness, there is an indispensable order to
maintain the eternal circle.
You are seen as cause and seen as effect.
You are thought of as a cycle of evolution and creation.

Law,
Some have even created other names and concepts in a
pseudonym, such as "Law of the Jungle."
This is the false face of a daydreamer;
The product of their mind.

Significance,
As in the actual jungle, the powerful prey upon the weak;
they see it as a matter of fact, their right, nature's
requirement to continuous existence.
It is such with the self-centered and greedy, who believe
everything is their natural right, but in the jungle
there is no greed or conceit.

Therefore,
It is a fruitless comparison to look at human weaknesses as
Law, rather than what they are: rationalizations and
justifications to explain these weaknesses.

Law,
At this time more than ever it is a shame, and a sham of
what it was meant to be.
It has become a false reason for separation and human
pain and maladies.
It has become a dangerous false tool in the hand of cruel
and powerful rulers and the rich.
It is a source for prejudice in all sorts and forms.
It is still a dream in the mind of dreamers.

Volcano

We see and are conscious of the shining sun.
Everyday, in a continuous and hasty manner, it generously
    spreads its rays of light.
From time to time tall and short mountains erupt with
    rage and exasperation.

But!

The sun's light and heat are manifestations which give life
    splendor and luster,
While that of the volcano is a harshness that destroys and
    makes waste.
As clouds rain and give blessings for abundance and
    prosperity,
So too do volcanoes erupt and let fall a destructive and
    deadly rain of ash and fire.

On the other hand!

Rivers continuously moving along their route to the sea
    gratify the thirst of all things,
While the volcano's molten flood destroys and disappoints.

Analogy! It is the same in human nature.

One's motto is based on goodness and kindness,
  benevolence.
The other succeeds by stealing or cheating.
One person is in service to humanity and is happy with
  the joy of sincerity.
The other lives with crime and villainy.

So!

If the day comes when the children of man can harness
  volcanoes,
It is certain then they can also change the nature of the
  causes of human wickedness.
And if the day comes when the children of man can
  harness all other destructive forces of the universe,
  like floods or earthquakes,
It is certain then they can overcome the enemies of
  mankind, like those who live in sheepskins and show
  not their real selves.

It is on that day that neither the volcanoes shall willfully
  destroy,
Nor in any corner of the world shall anyone lose their life
  to the headstrong or the greedy.

The Sun

O lustrous seal over the sky.
O luminous star in the miscellanea of the world,
You, O kind and glowing star,
That your parental affection is all inclusive,
And your generous virtue is scattered
Upon all the world's inhabitants.
You are that all the small and the great,
Of any color and composition,
With any conviction or object,
Are equal and revered at your side.
So also that your life-giving radiation sheds a ray of
        affection
And a cry for justice upon all hearts and minds
Until the roots of separation and hypocrisy,
Hatred and hostility,
All totally could be burned and made to disappear.
Afterwards, with a profound transformation,
The dignity and splendor of humanity,
The temperament, disposition, and grandiose majesty of
        mankind,
And the prosperity of people for all ages
Will have blown into them a fresh, new spirit,
And from their character and faces
The light of purity will come sparkling.

The Ecstasy of the First Kiss

I have attended many celebrations for all sorts of
        happenings,
But this was the first celebration for the Kiss.
And it became my most memorable celebration.

The daintiness and enjoyment of that Kiss brought forth
        the
Lifelong ecstasy of my subconscious, suckling milk from
        the breast.

The hour that we lay side by side in each other's arms had
        the
Tranquility, calmness, and quiet of springtime in a forest.

When we had our hands entwined, holding each other in
Life-giving gentleness will be an everlasting memory.
And I still feel its dampness.

As I was speaking, with only a look meaning more
Penetrating than words came from deep within your mind
    and heart.
Your powerful, kind, generous, and loving heart was
    beating with a penetrating speed.

Your joyous and rose-colored face with its warmth still
    burns on my face,
When my glance fell on your legs, knees, calves, ankles,
I saw the essence of art known to artists through the ages.

Then I knew what caused idolatry, and it was the same
    whether I saw you coming toward me or going away.

How Could It Be Possible?

How could it be possible?
    To renounce attachment from your true love.
    Isn't that the lowest of thoughts whenever such a
        choice is made?

How could it be possible?
    To leave and forget good friends.
    Isn't that as bats hiding in the caves, deprived of
        beauty visible only in the light?

How could it be possible?
    To keep one's mouth shut and hands crossed on the
        chest in confrontation of injustice.
    Isn't that a choice of vileness made without just or
        selfless thought?

How could it be possible?
    To pay homage to power, money, and position,
        striving to achieve these for personal gain.
    Isn't that a trait of the cowardly opportunists, the
        self-centered, the betrayers of society?

How could it be possible?
    To confuse physical pain with the sorrows of life.
    Isn't that a sign of a confused mind, or the mind of an
        attention seeker?

How could it be possible?
    To accumulate and increase money, fortune,
        possessions through cheating and fraud.
    Isn't that a characteristic of leeches, aren't these
        human leeches?

How could it be possible?
    To waste life with aimlessness and trivia.
    Isn't that a betrayal of the virtues nature has given us?

How could it be possible?
    To accept the crow's song in place of the canary or
        nightingale's melody.
    Isn't that as coming from a monotonous and
        unexposed mind?

All are possible!
    If you grow and learn without the lessons of
        childhood love.
    If you have been suppressed and abused.
    If you are taught to value greediness.

A Mother's Message

Oh, dear child, listen to some of my thoughts.
Don't suppose it is to oblige you and don't suppose I am
      giving advice,
But it is such as the mirror that gives a true image.
With honesty and sincerity I would like to say a few
      simple deep-hearted words to touch your emotions
      and to stir understanding in your heart and mind.
I speak with the feelings of an inspired musician.

Yes, dear child,
Every woman can be a mother in the sense of delivering,
      breast-feeding, and caring for a child through all the
      growth periods, from infancy through youth, until the
      child is given to society.
All mothers can progress with their child through these
      stages, but if one looks more deeply into the level of
      caring and nurturing,
Not all mothers and fathers are the same,
As not all children are the same.

My dear child,
Remember the past and give testimony to it.
I was a mother obsessed with nurturing you fully
And, without exaggeration, wanting to do my best I
      sacrificed my youth and everything for your
      well-being.
And hereafter I will continue to live with your concerns
      and love in mind.

Because I have hope and confidence in your success and
     grace,
Now, oh you, my bright and luminous candle,
Oh you, my life extract and power,
For all that I have so generously given, with great
     expectation and hopefulness, I ask in return that you:

—Guard and preserve your physical and mental health
     and not contaminate yourself with undesirable habits,
     vices or obsessions;
—Seek knowledge and wisdom and be ravenous in this
     quest;
—Follow the road most lawful and legitimate in the
     accumulation of wealth and fortune, and be laborious.

Humans in this age more than ever need wisdom and
     perception;
Lacking these they are not accountable to the cause of
     justice.
Likewise, a learned and scholarly person who is
     moneyless and empty-handed is without credit and
     positive influence.
And as I leave this world, I will keep this hope alive; that
     you will be true to all as long as you live,
That you will have a prosperous life and all your wishes
     will come true.

Procession of the Flowers

Spring is here, and a procession of flowers is blooming in
     every direction.
The spring rains have cleansed all that was dirty.
Earth has taken off her white robe, removing the glassy,
     cold cover from her body,
And in its place she adorns herself with leaves, flowers,
     buds—a new garment.
The wrathful thunder and lightning have ceased and gone
     away.
So come, while it's still possible, let us wash our unhappy
     faces with dew in which the flower petals float.
From the corner of the room, the closed, tight quarters
     where you have been staying,
Come out; walk with the headiness of ecstasy and enjoy
     the miracles of nature.
You are a part of them.
If then, a sweet smile does not appear on your lips and
     your whole person does not show cheerfulness,
Without a doubt all other creatures will think you have a
     brittle and unchangeable nature.
The perfection of creation, for those who see it with
     insight, will increase their ability to see even deeper.
As with the greenness of nature, search for and find a new
     face.

At any moment in time that your route passes a garden, or
a space of untouched nature,
Try to pick up the breeze of joy and the natural high
produced by nature's unadulterated perfume.
The season of the flowers is short-lived, as are all of
nature's breathtaking effects.
The truth is that they are even more short-lived than can
be conceived.
But only when miracles appear, can they attract the hearts
that are capable of falling in love,
Like the period of life when love, hope, and dreams are
first observed by the young.
Yes, it is sweet to spend time walking in nature, on the
plains, in the hills or mountains, especially in the
springtime.
It is even better if we have our love with us, to talk and
share in the sweetness, to be a companion and sharer
of joys.
A real love is the ultimate of ecstasy.
That which we do not realize until it is absent from us.
So, let us look at the newcomer, at the wind and breeze
and rain of spring,
And congratulate the procession of the flowers in the
gardens, and in their majesty the miracles of nature.

The Trap and the Bait

Oh, Sweetheart, your gaze toward me is often that of a
	stranger,
And yet other times it is a measure of grace and kindness.

It is the energy of Life in those ruby-colored lips;
The arch of your eyebrows represents both the trap and
	the bait.

When you breathe, your nose gives off breath like that of a
	messiah,
While your cheeks are as soft as the down on a butterfly's
	wings.

The fine, crystalline shape of your neck asks gently to be
	stroked,
And the dimple of your chin is a wonder to watch and to
	touch.

Your figure, so delicate, makes even the fairies jealous,
And your nature is one of queenly compassion and mercy.

Your smile is so expressive it communicates without
    words,
And each wordless message is a rare and incomparable
    gem.

Your moments of silence are so filled with energy and life,
My own life I would sacrifice in total adoration.

I become lighthearted when you are with me or on my
    mind.
It is the ultimate of Life and Luck you have given me.

Teacher

The beauty of life is to be of service to others.
This idea has been echoed through the ages by all who
have influenced mankind's life and thought.

Yes, universal reality of this idea will give life more value,
more worth.
But if it does not exist, where there are bad deeds, there is
foulness.

For whoever has this knowledge, it becomes guidance and
they shall know
That man's fruit is in helpfulness and fellowship.

Yes!

It is true the value of external beauty is a temporary
pleasure.
It is also true that attraction to fortune, position, and
physical beauty all are temporary pleasures that
humans strive for, and on most occasions find
necessary.
But, kindness in life is true beauty.

Proposition:
This true beauty, long-lasting beauty, when mixed with
    helpfulness to others makes life more valued and
    fruitful.

That is so.

The effect of this service is visible, measurable,
Its fruits everlasting, and its current goes from generation
    to generation.

Question:
What service? Should we choose one over another?

Proposition:
What is nobler than educating the children? A balance of
    formal and informal education will manifest itself
    through the ages as service to society.

Who could be more useful and helpful to society and the
    world at large?
Who are the rocks, the foundations of humanity's progress?

It is the teacher who truly influences a child's life. It is the
    teacher who can direct a young mind, regardless of its
    roots, to a constructive path.

It is the teacher who prepares children for life and service
    to others.
Each new idea, concept, or simple word is a door the
    teacher opens to children.

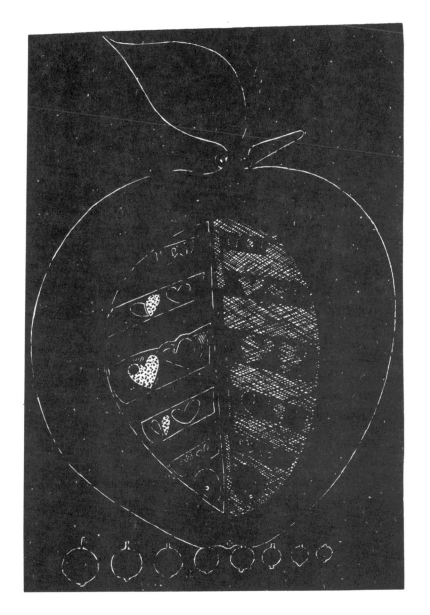

Those whose job through the years is teaching in whatever capacity should climb on society's shoulders.

You, Teachers, are the creators and nurturers of wisdom and knowledge.

You, Teachers, have fostered and nourished all of science and history.

You, Teachers, are the truest and most sincere friends of humanity.

You, Teachers, are the most honest and respected followers of perception and knowledge.

You, Teachers, are the most qualified heirs of the prophets, philosophers, and scientists, whose work and sacrifices have through the ages given guidance and direction to the nations.

Then long live your name,
Long live your actions,
May your message be everlasting.

Whoever you are,
Wherever you live,
Whatever you are thinking.

Know Yourself

Oh, you, who are absorbed in a sea of vanity and
    drunkenness,
Oh, you, who are lost in the desert of lust, passion and
    egotism,
Oh, you, who have plunged into the slimy marsh of
    vileness and meanness,

> Take time to be introspective until you at last come to
>   your senses,
> If you are not already intoxicated.

Oh, you, the flower in the entire flock of all the living
    creatures,
Oh, you, discoverer of the many secrets and mysteries of
    life,
Oh, you, inventor of that which is novel, artistic, or
    unknown,

> Take time to be introspective until you at last come to
>   your senses,
> If you are not already intoxicated.

Oh, you, who are enamoured with the love of violence,
    war and dispute,
Oh, you, manufacturer of the tools of war, arms and
    deadly weapons,
Oh, you, the burden to be borne on the shoulders of the
    wronged, the oppressed,

> Take time to be introspective until you at last come to
>   your senses,
> If you are not already intoxicated.

How long are you in this state of lethargy, in this sleep of
  ignorance?
How long have you been so miserly, concerned with
  finding silver and gold?
How long have you been evil and wicked; how long unjust
  and oppressive?

> Take time to be introspective until you at last come to
>   your senses,
> If you are not already intoxicated.

If you are enlightened, you can do without illusions and
  mimicry.
If you are freehearted, you have no restrictions; you do not
  defile life.
So it is, I remind you of the wishes of all the centuries:

> Take time to be introspective until you at last come to
>   your senses,
> If you are not already intoxicated.

45

Seeking Luck

What should I make of you? Whatever it is will surely
    wound my heart.
What should I say to you? Whatever I say will be either
    too much or too little.
Ecstasy and sorrow both exude from you.
What can I expect of you? Whatever I expect will bring me
    anxiety.
Yesterday is past and tomorrow is unknown.
What questions can I ask you? Whatever I ask will be
    either about the past or the future.
O, Luck, where are you in my life? Why don't you come
    looking for me?
What should I seek from you? Whatever I seek, should I
    feel it is something you owe me?

Flowing Water

Rivulets of water change into flowing streams,
Streams into small rivers,
Small rivers become mighty rivers,
And the mighty rivers empty themselves into open waters.

Reflection
Are these flowing waters obedient components of nature,
Or are they some lost and headstrong entities?
Do they represent the steps of growth, development and
    maturity,
Or the law of nature that separate parts should join to
    become the whole?

Proposition
Sit for a moment beside a brook
And observe the passage of life.
You will see that water, in addition to being life-giving and
    the guarantor of survival,
Also represents the movement of life with its endless
    passage.

Yes! Water flows and life passes.
Happiness is for those who grab ahold of every drop or
    moment;
And their spirits will not depart to the marsh
As does wasted water.

Enamored

My idol, I knew you would leave me, but why so soon?
What made you not want to fulfill your promises?

My eyes and my heart had been as a mirror in front of you.
You put me aside and with that removed your reflection
    from me. Why?

When I wanted to look with full satisfaction into your
    magical and mesmerizing eyes,
What made you close your eyes and frown?

When I held you in my arms and lovingly embraced your
    life-giving body,
What made you take yourself away, if you didn't intend to
    refuse me or withhold from me?

When you were leaving for what I thought was to be a
    temporary absence, I wanted to kiss you.
You bit your lip and went out the door.
What makes you be so cruel?

As soon as I looked at your queenly stature, with all its
    grace and freedom,
What made you start to strut?

I was not aware that I was so deeply absorbed by my love
    for you.
I am losing my life. What makes you not want to fill my
    vase?

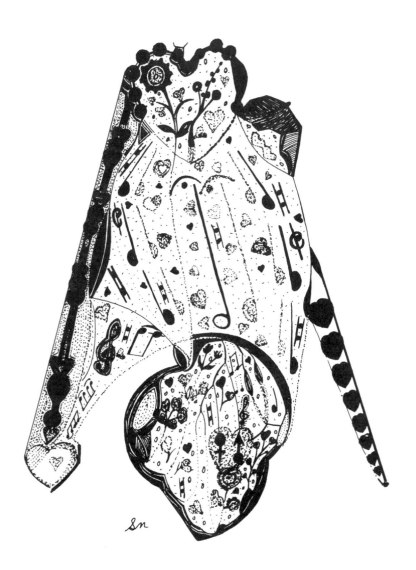

My satisfaction had been in harmony with your existence.
What made you untie this knot and let me fall?

After hundreds of tests, still I would hear your cold
    responses.
If you would have me repeat the tests, it would have been
    enough. What made you reject me?

I am prepared to live and burn in your love continuously.
O, you, the physician for all my pain,
What makes you talk about cure and recovery?

I Come from the Jungle

I come from the jungle.
Where the soil is covered with weeds, dry grass, herbs,
    and forage;
Where in every season wild flowers on all sides and in
    every corner present a special parade;
Where thick and luxuriant trees with their heavenly sphere
    stand strong against any assault or aggression.

I come from the jungle.
That infinite space that is fascinating and desirable, whose
    life-giving air is so agreeable that it spreads its grace
    for miles within its borders;
That place where every particle of leaf, fruit, and branch is
    used by all in one way or another throughout the
    seasons;
That place whose gardener is nature herself and whose
    irrigator is every pregnant cloud.

I come from the jungle.
The home whose history is longer than that of almost any
    other being on earth;
The home which is the principal birthplace of nearly all
    that lives on earth;
The home whose open and eager embrace has nurtured
    and raised our ancestors.

Introspection.
Yes, I come from surroundings where trees young and old,
    tall and short, fruitful and fruitless create no problems
    for one another, and instead exist in long rows of
    intricate arrangements, together in complete peace
    and serenity.

Yes, I come from that place where each occupant
    generously and fully serves the needs of every other,
    giving refuge to all and honoring whatever they
    desire to rest and to live.

And I often wonder about man's continued destructive
    relationship with nature.
Will the jungle be there at all the next time I return,
    and if it is there, will it be the same as when I left?

My Dear Child

My dear child,
I think about you and am joyful and content.

I see in you my own mold or recall myself in your face.
That within you exists the secrets of my youth
And your own success and grace completes my happiness.

My dear child,
I think about you and am joyful and content.

I ask that you endeavor to be clever and wise.
Meditate and discover with your inner eyes
That your heart beats whether you wish for it or not.
Then, lucky is the one who enjoys more,
And whose every day is better than the one before.

My dear child,
I think about you and am joyful and content.

That the son is a young father who is energetic and able,
And the father in turn is a sagacious son.
Then wish to heaven that you be like me, but much more.
That in the not too distant future I will be as you are, full of
    effort and art.

My dear child,
I think about you and am joyful and content.

You that from the warm and protected embrace of your
    mother
Are like a bird sent out to the universe,
And she, as I, continuously has your face in her eyes, and
    talks about your behavior and desires,

And has everlasting love.

Momentary Absorption

Your kiss today has become more grasping and absorbing,
Your laughter has become more alluring and charming,
With those winsome glances which are filled with tumult.

The elegance of your appearance has become more
    fascinating and charming
Since you loosened your curls over your shoulder.
Your stature, like a weeping willow tall as a cypress, has
    become most graceful.
Even more than the butterfly's wing or the blossom's petal,
Your skin is elegant, soft, and delicate.
Your cheeks are as ripe red pomegranate jewels.

What can I say?
Your face today has become more fascinating and beautiful.

Now that you know what you are and what I feel,
Please have a less mincing air of coquettish endearment.
Alas! Who do you remember or expect to see who is more
    distracted with love for you than me?

The Horizon

I love the horizon.
The horizon, all that is farthest and most open.
The horizon, so full of stars, the more stars the better.

The ancient people believed that the stars were visible
    signs of the fortunes of man.

A second idea is to see the horizon as an ocean,
Whose waves are the glittering of the stars.
Undoubtedly, the whole then reflects the conditions of the
    fortunate.
With this description, all that is horizon is even more
    spacious and far-reaching,
And the possibility of viewing the luck of the fortunate is
    greater.

Another point of view is of a man with pure and honest
    virtues.
Such a man's thoughts are for all, and he considers the
    goodness of humankind, regardless of anything else.
This virtuous man wishes for everyone's star to glow—to
    the end of time.

So let us all look at the horizon with praise and adoration.
The horizon, all that is farthest and most open.
The horizon, so full of stars, the more stars the better.

The Valley of My Love

In the land of my love, the wings of the birds are so rich in beauty and color that any comparison would be to taunt the wings of the angels.

The soil on which she walks is finer and more splendid than the most precious jewels; the larger stones and rocks exceed the splendor of the crown jewels of the world's most powerful royalty.

In this land, her voice, her walk, her every movement and expression are more awesome and majestic than those of mythical figures.

The most sacred temples do not capture the people's attention or their souls as my love's territory, that universal point of attention and longing.

The vision and wisdom in her land is so overwhelming that it surpasses all the world's sages.

It is such an everlasting land of love and unity of existence that a million words or even documents cannot express it.

In the refuge of her love and affection, there is no
   discrimination of race, sex, age, or religion.

As she moves, the motion of the air is more refreshing than
   the breezes of paradise, to a point that the air becomes
   animated.

Ah, the land of my love is a paradise where all beings seek
   everlasting life, where no one need fear danger or
   surprise.

It is the desire of all souls to be granted entrance, one by
   one, into this valley of love, honor, and happiness.

Without You

You left, and without you an endless spring of tears
    remains.
My heart grieves as if it contains a single burning ember.

The tears pouring onto my lap are like shining jewels,
    falling continuously.
Of all the happiness, joy and ecstasy you brought, only
    fantasy and dreams remain.

Yesterday, with my healthy heart and mind, I was like the
    strongest tree.
Today there is a sickly spruce in its place.

The Garden of Life was filled with millions of flowers in
    your presence,
But now only empty branches are left scattered about.

Peace, best wishes, compassion, songs and joy
All become fiction without you, replaced by wickedness
    and disorder.

Every spring your beauty brought paradise to earth;
However, this year the appearance of spring is just that.

Without the presence of a sweetheart in paradise there is
    no reason even to pause.
I am burning from your departure and only ashes are left.

My fear is that after all this hope, you will return too late,
When wings and dust will be all that remain of this
burning, enamored butterfly.

Yet, why such expectation for despair?
If tenderness and love return, in its presence one will
suddenly transform into complete perfection.

Looking at You

O! Clear and immaculate, crisp air raining sparks on my
  breast,
Tell grief and anxiety of the heart to go from here as soon
  as possible.
Give assistance to my life, cleanse from my blood any
  inpurity.
Firmly fix joy, happiness, and the light of hope in my inner
  self.

O! Lamp of heaven, a seal of love and affection
Who shines with pleasure upon the sons of man.
Illumination is of you, and your wrath spreads darkness.
Your ray, no matter how fiery, resembles your poignant
  love for me, so shine and increase to eternity my
  tranquility and peace.

O! Tears of the azure dome, rain fine drops upon the farms.
Whatever in the world moves, you are the sign of its
  excitement.
Could you transform into a flood that could destroy
  completely the foundation of hatred and revenge?

O! Good-looking portrait in the moon which resembles my
  lover's attraction,
When you appear it makes every eye calm, eyes that have
  been searching continuously for you.
Never hide your face behind a dark cloud.
Every night of my life be full, your face the light and giver
  of life.

The Day of True Love

The day of true love, the day of the enamored, the day of
the attached.
Oh, what a happy day; what a full-of-grandeur day!
If only lovers of all ages could feel it throughout their
senses and in everything within the universe,
That who is the creator of nobility and excellence is one
who is the follower of such delicate philosophy and
belief.

Proposition
To be an eager lover or witness of pure love of others.

Proposition
That ecstasy and delight come from the warm busses of a
true lover.

Introspection
It can elate the lover to purity in worship and pleasure in
martyrdom.

Option
A clear smile on the face and internal absorption of the
soul of the charmed.
It is truthful kindness with life-giving affection and the
symbol of chastity of my heart and soul.

Introspection
Isn't that what we offer to our true lover?

And oh, would to heaven you, the benevolent and the
    humanist, establish love as a universal human value
    and it be an epidemic;
And everyone in every corner of the earth would be as a
    true and pure lover, with the good nature which
    encompasses all in such a day.

The day of true love
A day that is every day with entrance into the souls of
    others through the means of the senses: touch, sight,
    smell, taste, sound,

Until their kindness has established the strongest roots,
    their relationships the warmest and with the deepest
    foundation;
Until their oneness and uniqueness is the sturdiest.

Is it simplistic to therefore expect a universal love based on
    peace and compromise with no one as the better or
    conqueror for whatsoever reason,
To live in harmony and with love?

Affirmation
Is such a day and place too much to expect?
Is such a day and place only in a dreamer's world?
Is such a place a better world?
Will such a day last?
Would such a world increase the will for life?
Is such a world more fruitful and prosperous?
All these questions and more will be easy to answer if such
    a day comes and such a place exists.

Introspection
I wonder, what would incite us to move toward such a day,
Is it going to be our eventual universal misery or
    prosperity?

Proposition
For whatever will assist us to this end, hope exists and this
    hope will be eternal.

The day of true love, the day of the enamored, the day of
    the attached.
Oh, what a happy day; what a full-of-grandeur day!
If only lovers of all ages could feel it throughout their
    senses and in everything within the universe,
That who is the creator of nobility and excellence is one
    who is the follower of such delicate philosophy and
    belief.

Extremes in Similarities

An unlucky day and one of happiness and gratification are
both days, but what a difference.
A shot from a bow and a glance from my lover's eyes are
both penetrating, but what a difference.
Living to endeavor for progress or living inaccessibly are
both ways of living, still what a difference.
Having aspiration to receive knowledge or making every
effort to accumulate wealth are both accepted, but
what a difference.
A corrupt politician and an honest one are both leaders,
but what a difference.
A starving man and one who has access to food can both
feel hunger, but what a difference.

Aging and Oldness

As white dust settles on one's head, it is customary to call
that person old.
But how often it takes a long passage of time before aging
becomes oldness,
As one by one all the senses, the power, and the body's
natural defenses encounter disorder
And, like infants, need necessitates the individual be cared
for and looked after.
With this distinction:
An infant neither knows how nor is able to care for itself,
While the old person knows how but is not able.
An infant is fresh and cheerful, in search of knowledge and
self-sufficiency;
The aged is moving toward disintegration, forgetfulness,
and the loss of knowledge.
Everyone likes and wants to help care for the infant;
But, more often than not, they may dislike the aged and
help only out of pity.
The infant is growing into society, becoming active and
useful within the group;
While the aged has begun to slow down, to stop trying, to
end the search.
Yes, this is the story of the old, who suffer so much,
regardless of money, earthly possessions, experience,
knowledge, or humor.